>>> **THE** ~~

OFFICE

Bollocks

THIS IS A PRION BOOK

This reduced edition first published in Great Britain in 2016 by Prion
An imprint of the Carlton Publishing Group
20 Mortimer Street
London W1T 3JW

Hardback edition published in 2016

A CIP catalogue for this book is available from the British Library.

ISBN 978-1-85375-965-9

Printed in Dubai

10 9 8 7 6 5 4 3 2 1

THE _{LITTLE} BOOK OF

(title reads: THE LITTLE BOOK OF)

OFFICE

Bollocks

Banish Monday-to-Friday, 9-to-5 office boredom!

MALCOLM CROFT

OFFICE HACKS

PRION

CORPORATE BUZZWORD BINGO

Dear Office Drone,

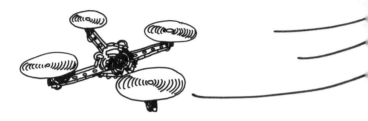

Let's be honest, office life is ridiculous. Which, I'm afraid to say, means your life is ridiculous.

You spend 40 hours a week cramped in a dank, unchallenging and unrewarding atmosphere just so you can go home at the end of a long week unsatisfied, underpaid and riddled with repetitive strain injury and pointless anxiety. So you eat. And drink. To numb the pain.

Humans, as we all know, are simply not built to sit on their butts all day, burning out our retinas staring at a spreadsheet, completely squandering the potential that more than 700 million years of glorious evolution has given us.

As the old joke goes, you work in an office for 40 years of your life – you get less for murder. Though, of course, if you work in an office, you'll have daydreamed about stapling a colleague to their desk and bludgeoning them over the head repeatedly with a QWERTY keyboard, or garroting them with a mouse cable.

So, if you're reading this at your desk, instead of working, then good for you! That's exactly what this book is about. This book is a two-fingered salute to work, a flip of the bird to The Man, and a hearty raspberry right in the face of Corporate Officedom.

If you are currently employed and show up to work at an office, if you spend the hours between nine and five sat at a cold and often cramped desk, if you are surrounded by other miserable people you can't stand to look at, let alone talk to – you are not alone. Look to your left. That person – as annoying as they might be – is probably just as miserable as you.

By simply buying/stealing/borrowing/regifting this book, you have taken one small step into a simpler world, a world where middle managers don't exist, where computers don't need rebooting 30 times a day, where office politics is a thing that exists only in nightmares, and staff meetings are just a figment of the Devil's imagination. By admitting that you have a problem – that your office life is rubbish – we can begin to work together to solve the problem and end corporate lunacy once for all.

Welcome to your new world order. Now, spend two hours making a cup of tea, and let's all get to work thinking about how we can leave work early tonight without anyone noticing…

Obvious Disclaimer

The publishers of this humorous book will not be held liable if you are dumb enough to actually carry out some of the dumb stuff contained within. You have been warned.

The Small print

I, the undersigned, agree that by picking up a copy of this book am taking action to demonstrate that I hate my office job – not necessarily because of the actual role I worked hard at university to qualify for, but because of the negatively charged office environment I am forced to endure day in, day out. And the incompetent idiots I must endure: their small-mindedness, arrogance and egomaniacal behaviour, and the counter-productive politics which threaten to ruin not only this company, but also all humankind in one swift death knell.

I, the undersigned, hereby reject and denounce the devil's suffocating control at [*insert your company's name here*] and, from this point on, promise to not care about staff meeting minutes, document scanning, passive/aggressive leaving cards and mindless office gossip.

Please, please make my wildest dreams come true. I cannot stand to work another second in this evil temple of doom.

_____

[*sign name here*]

Quote Quota #83

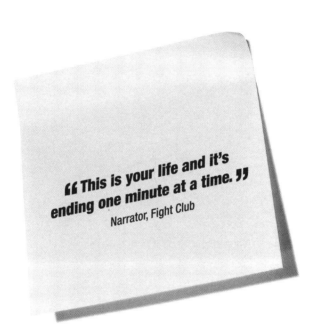

" This is your life and it's ending one minute at a time. "

Narrator, Fight Club

Lies Lies Lies

A 2014 survey of jobseekers in the UK reported how six out of ten people admitted lying or exaggerating on their CV in order to boost their chances of a first interview. It also reported that 16 per cent falsely claimed to speak another language and 27 per cent "embellished" their IT skills. Hands up… was it you?

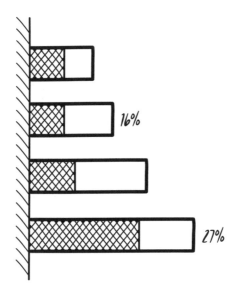

Top CV Lies

We all lie on our CVs, right? Here are the most common porkies… and their inconvenient truths:

1 **"I have a First Class degree"**
I got a 2:1, but I was one per cent away from a first, so I always just round up.

2 **"I love to travel"**
I went to France with my parents in school holidays.

3 **"I've never been fired from a job"**
Please don't ask me to explain the six-month gap in my employment history.

4 **"My previous role was Assistant Regional Manager"**
My previous role was Assistant to the Regional Manager.

5 **"I'm passionate about digital marketing"**
I want to get paid loads of money just to sit around and search Facebook all day.

6 **"I enjoy spending time with my friends and exploring the city I live in"**
I like to get drunk with my mates and hang out in as many pubs as possible.

7 **"I am advanced in most computer software programmes"**
I can use Word and Excel, a bit, the rest I'll just pick up. How hard can it be?

8 **"I increased profit at my company by 7 per cent"**
I was part of a team that reported profits had risen while I was working there.

9 **"I pay attention to the details"**
The word "details" was spelt wrong in all previous drafts of this CV.

#1 Playlist
How To Make It
Through Monday

Hung-over? Tired? Skint? Anxiety-riddled? Yep, that sounds like Monday.
This playlist will help ease you in to the working week…

▶ 1. **Mo Money Mo Problems – The Notorious B.I.G.**

▶ 2. **Opportunities (Let's Make Lots of Money) –
Pet Shop Boys**

▶ 3. **Don't Talk To Me About Work – Lou Reed**

▶ 4. **Seven Days of the Week (I Never Go To Work) –
They Might Be Giants**

▶ 5. **I Don't Like Mondays – The Boomtown Rats**

▶ 6. **Working Class Hero – John Lennon**

▶ 7. **Slave to the Grind – Skid Row**

▶ 8. **Just Another Manic Monday – The Bangles**

▶ 9. **Hard Knock Life – Jay Z**

▶ 10. **A Hard Day's Night – The Beatles**

Office History #1:
The Office Chair

Don't waste time clock-watching while sat at your desk. That's boring. Instead, waste time reading the paragraph below. It's both boring and fascinating at the same time.

The one thing you'll spend the rest of your life sitting on – the humble office chair – was actually invented by Charles Darwin, in the 1800s. Yes, *that* Charles Darwin. For those of you who went to school, he needs no introduction. For the rest (majority?) of you, Charles Darwin was the man who changed the world by theorizing, correctly as it turned out, that all life has evolved from previous species. He also invented the office chair. Amazingly, Darwin was the first bright spark to add wheels to the legs of his laboratory chair – so, we assume, he could zoom around to observe his exotic platypus specimens more quickly.

Like I said, boring and fascinating.

Office Dares #2: Emojis

Emojis are everywhere these days, people are getting sick of them. Next time you want to pull a sickie, why not use an emoji to tell your boss you're not feeling very well. Like so…

-----------Original Message-------------
From: jsmith@workworkwork.com
Sent: Thursday, 11 June 2015, 09.15am
Subject: Feeling unwell

Dear [*insert name of boss*],

I am feeling 😵 **and** 👎
I'll head to the 🏥 **if I don't feel any better.**
I wont come to the office for fear of
Will stay at 🏠
Thanks,

Top Ten: Fonts To Glamourize Dull Work Emails

If you really want to piss off your co-workers – and you really should want to – then these are the greatest fonts to use in serious communications to really achieve that objective. They add a little spice to the otherwise meaningless corporate jargon you have to send. Best used at point size 18.

1 Curlz MT

2 **BLACKOAK STD**

3 **MARKER FELT**

4 Edwardian Script ITC

5 DESDEMONA

6 **ROSEWOOD STD**

7 ZAPFINO

8 Handwriting - Dakota

9 Lucida Handwriting

10 **BRAGGADOCIO**

REMEMBER:

Nothing says, "I'm completely serious about the work I do" than…using COMIC SANS MS in *all* your work emails. Try it out. You'll be fired by the end of the day.

Top 5: Out Of Office Messages

Out of Office messages are so dull. Wouldn't it be great if we could jazz them up a little...with the truth!

-----------Original Message------------
From: jsmith@workworkwork.com
Sent: Wednesday, 24 December 2015, 09.00am
Subject: Christmas Eve

My body may physically present in the office today, but my mind, soul and spirit, is already out the door… and has been since 01 December.

Your email will now not be read until January 03.

If your query is urgent…tough sh*t. You should have sent it to me sooner.

Happy Holidays.

-----------Original Message------------
From: jsmith@workworkwork.com
Sent: Friday, 16 January 2015, 3:05pm
Subject: Out Of Office

I am currently out of the office.

If you wish for your email to be placed at the top of my inbox for when I return, please press your thumb on the hyperlink below.
CLICK HERE*

*Clicks through to www.Hotbottoms.co.uk

-----------Original Message------------
From: jsmith@workworkwork.com
Sent: Friday, 16 January 2015, 3:05pm
Subject: Out Of Office

Hi, I'm Troy McClure. You might remember me from such previous Out of Office Messages as I've Gone to a Dentist's Appointment that Definitely Exists And Is Not A Job interview, and I'm Not Feeling Very Well...But It Has Nothing To Do With Getting Drunk Last Night.

-----------Original Message------------
From: jsmith@workworkwork.com
Sent: Friday, 16 January 2015, 3:05pm
Subject: Out Of Office

I am out of the office until 17/11/16. I will be unable to delete all the emails you send me until I return from my well-deserved holiday away from you idiots. Rest assured your email will be deleted in the order it was received.

Thanks.

-----------Original Message------------
From: jsmith@workworkwork.com
Sent: Tuesday, 11 June 2015, 17.29pm
Subject: Holiday Handover

I am now on holiday for two weeks. I will not be reading my emails while I am away.

I also "forgot" to do a handover holiday form. I sort of got the feeling that none of you cared about my work.

Have fun talking about me while I'm away. Thanks.

Quote Quota #19

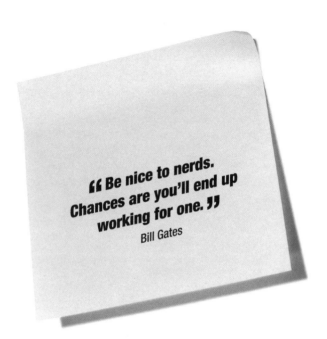

❝ Be nice to nerds. Chances are you'll end up working for one. ❞

Bill Gates

Speaking In Code

A brilliant way to waste time at work is to devise a code system with a mate or your partner, where work-related words and phrases can be substituted for non-working words. By doing this, you can make a "personal call" sound a lot like a "work call". Here are some beginner code words to get you started:

WORD	CODEWORD
Working hard	How are you doing?
Busy right now	How was your evening last night?
Completing objectives	Bored of Facebook for today
Meeting targets	What are you doing this weekend?
Working late	Fancy meeting at 5.30 sharp for a beer?
Global economic crisis	I'm getting really drunk tonight
Deadline looming	I'm not doing any work today
Client facing	What are you wearing?
Hungry for results	What are we having for dinner?
Goal orientated	Is there football on tonight?
Require extra incentives	I'll nick some toilet paper from the office toilet

Obviously, if you want longer conversations, you'll have to devise more code. But once you become fluent in the code, you'll be spending your whole day chatting "work" to your mate or partner without arousing suspicion. Alternatively, if this all just seems too much like hard work, then feel free to just make personal phone calls from your desk and see if anyone actually notices. Chances are, nobody gives a damn.

Top Ten Office Hates

There are many reasons why co-workers bicker and fight with each other: the kind of food we eat, how loud we talk on the phone, whether we stink of cigarettes or how much we kiss our boss's asses. While 44 per cent of people admitted to confronting their co-workers' bad habits, the rest of us appear to just accept that it's not part of the job.

WOMEN'S TOP TEN OFFICE HATES

1 Eating smelly food

2 Being late

3 Too many cigarette breaks

4 Bad hygiene

5 Not being organized

6 Messy desk

7 Colleagues not returning borrowed stationery

8 Talking on the phone too loudly

9 Taking too long for lunch

10 Dressing inappropriately

MEN'S TOP TEN OFFICE HATES

1 Messy desk

2 Colleagues spraying perfume or aftershave

3 Talking on the phone too loud

4 Being late

5 Taking too long for lunch

6 Eating smelly food

7 Too many cigarette breaks

8 Colleagues talking too much

9 Not being organized

10 Rudeness

Corporate Bollocks

This is wanky corporate jargon at its best. How many of these dreadful phrases have you said today?

BOLLOCKS	UNDERSTANDABLE
Going Forward	Progress
Idea Showers	Thinking
Incentivize	Blackmail / Manipulate
Product Evangelist	Believes in the product
Platform Atheist	Doesn't believe in the product
Touch Base	Communicate
Loop Back	Speak later
Low Hanging Fruit	Achievable Goal
360-degree thinking	Thinking
Close of Play	End of the Day
110 per cent	100 per cent (Quite a lot!)
Wrongside	Second guess

Quote Quota #5

❝Always be smarter than the people who hire you.❞
Lena Horne

Office Dare #6 –
Email Roulette

Open up a new email. Type in a swear word of your choice in the Subject Line. Click in the "Send To" line. Close your eyes. Type in any letter on the keyboard. Whoever's name pops up, send the email to them. No chickening out allowed.

Playlist – Post Appraisal Soundtrack

Do you sometimes wonder whose side your boss is on?

- ▶ 1. **Which Side Are You On? – Pete Seeger**
- ▶ 2. **Take This Job and Shove It – Johnny Paycheck**
- ▶ 3. **Feel Like A Number – Bob Seger**
- ▶ 4. **Shaddup You Face – Joe Dolce**
- ▶ 5. **I Can't Wait To Get Off Work – Tom Waits**
- ▶ 6. **The Ballad of Middle Management – The Breakers**
- ▶ 7. **Mixed Emotions – The Rolling Stones**
- ▶ 8. **Taking Care of Business – Bachman Turner Overdrive**
- ▶ 9. **This Is The Last Time – Keane**
- ▶ 10. **Must Have Done Something Right – Relient K**

Terms And Conditions Apply

Thirty-five per cent of the world's workforce loathes their job. If you've had enough of working long hours for little pay and no reward, then fill out an application form for the world's easiest jobs today:

1. **Lifeguard** (no-one hardly ever needs saving, let's be honest)

2. **Sports mascot** (working in fancy dress – what's not to love?)

3. **Living statue** (you literally get paid to do nothing)

4. **Ice cream man** (scoop ice cream into a cone, drive around and repeat. Job done)

5. **Cat sitter** (sit with a cat, get paid, go home)

6. **Buckingham Palace Guard** (your only job requirement is to stand there and do nothing.)

Office Dares #8 –
Make A Voodoo Doll
Of Your Boss

A great way to waste ten minutes of your day is to collect as much Blu-Tack as possible from around the office and to sculpt it into a Voodoo Doll that bares a great resemblance to your manager, or a co-worker you despise. A great way to ensure a strong sense of likeness is to buy a *Star Wars* toy figure (1:6 ratio) – Han Solo is the best if your boss is a man, Princess Leia if she is female – and cover the toy in Blu-Tack until it resembles a blue human figure. Now you are free to dress and decorate the figure to match your enemy, but the sharp notice board pins you use stay in nice and firmly when you poke the doll repeatedly in the groin.

Office Dares #111 –
Mug Fun

After someone sends out an all-staff email asking "if anyone has seen my mug...", go on a mission around the office to help find the mug. Once located, hide it. Hide it in a place where it will never be found. Then laugh maniacally to yourself, like this: "Muah, hah, hah, hah, hah, muah, hah, hah, muah, hah, hah," and so on...

Office Toilet Commandments

These are the only rules of the office that you are never allowed to bend or break…

1 Never poo in a urinal

2 Never wee in the sink

3 Never write graffiti on the toilet door (people will recognize your handwriting)

4 Always refill the toilet roll if it runs out on your watch

5 Always scrub the porcelain – no brown streaks or stains allowed

6 Never leave wee on the seat

7 Never talk about work while standing at a urinal next to a colleague

8 Never make small chat with the person sat in the cubicle next to yours

9 Never spend more than ten minutes sitting down

10 Always open the window

Golden Rule: If you can smell your own, it's ten times worse for everyone else.

Signs That You May Be Going Mad

They say you don't need to be mad to work in an office, but it helps. But what if you genuinely are driving yourself mad? Watch out for these symptoms.

1 You call your manager "Mum"

2 You can't remember if today is Tuesday or Wednesday

3 You buy the same super expensive coffee from the same coffee shop every day simply because it's the closest one to your office

4 You can't remember how you got to work

5 You can't remember getting home from work

6 You get angry when someone else uses "your" coffee mug

7 You take only ten minutes for lunch – even though legally you are allowed to take 60 minutes

8 You stay late to finish a piece of work that could easily be done the next day

9 You empathize with your co-workers

10 You have a "work husband or wife"

11 You start getting an early/later train into/from work to avoid the rush hour

12 You bring a plant to work and keep it on your desk. Effectively, you're nesting.

13 You stop buying toilet roll, because you know you can steal it from work

14 You tell your partner that you don't have the "bandwidth" to deal with their problems

15 You start noticing the clothing choices of your colleagues, and how often they wear certain items

Office-Related Cocktails – Part 1

Go ahead and make one (or all) of these home-made work-related cocktails, all guaranteed to dull the senses and slow the mind, just as if you were still stuck at your desk staring miserably at your monitor.

iDrink

A potent number to pay tribute to Apple Inc, whose time-wasting apps and tech make the working day a little easier to bear:

1 shot of whisky
1 shot of tequila
1 splash of coke
1 lemon squeeze
1 photo taken on an iPhone 6 and uploaded to Instagram

Printer jam

A sweet little treat to get you through an afternoon of photocopying:

2 shots of vodka
1 spoonful of strawberry jam, smoothed around the rim of the glass
1 error message (ignored)

The Intern (Non-Alcoholic)
Best to stay clear off:

1 shot of orange juice
1 wheatgrass shot chaser
1 early night

Xmas Party
This cocktail recipe is usually followed by the phrase "I'm never drinking again" the next morning:

3 shots dark rum
5 shots of tequila
2 glugs of someone's unwanted G&T
1 moment of regret

Your Office Is Literally Trying To Kill You Every Day

The air you breathe in your office is up to 100 times dirtier than the air you breathe outside... but sadly that's not the only thing in there that's trying to end your career as a living human being...

1 **Carbon Monoxide** – Look up. See a ventilation duct? That goes straight into a parking lot, where carbon monoxide from all the cars is now being pumped direct into your lungs.

2 **Black mould** – If your building is older than ten years, there will be black mould somewhere. Black mould releases Volatile Organic Chemicals which are toxic to humans – many thousands of office workers die of black mould poisoning worldwide every year.

3 **Ozone** – Do you ever walk over to the office photocopier or printer and think it smells funny? That's ozone and it's killing you. But don't worry: the manufacturers built in a filter to stop the ozone from leaking. When was the last time someone replaced the filter?

4 **Printer toner** – Your colour printer is emitting millions of tiny chemicals of toner into the air. These chemicals enter your bloodstream and lungs and increase your chances of cancer and heart disease. Scientists agree that breathing in toner is as bad as smoking a few cigarettes.

5 **Over-illumination** – Office fluorescent lighting gets a bad rep – and for good reason. It is killing you. Too much bright artificial light messes with our natural sleep cycles. Fluor-lighting, designed in the 1990s, was placed in most offices, as a way to increase productivity. But it can cause anxiety, migraines, stress, heart attacks and erectile dysfunction.

6 **Motivational Meetings** – Staff "fun" days out, team building exercises, motivational speakers – they are all designed to reinforce a positive attitude for your work and co-workers in the office space. It's bollocks. Scientists have proven that fake positivity is worse for your mental health than genuine negativity and can lead to depression.

7 **Boredom** – Boredom is the worst killer of all. Not only does boredom suck out your life force, increase lethargy and reduce empathy, it also puts you at a higher exposure to heart attack. By turning up, tuning in and dropping off at your dull office job, your heart rate decreases – meaning it won't work effectively when you need it to, such as, running away from the boss. Boredom also increases workplace accidents; your brain goes into autopilot mode, and doesn't react as quickly when you spill boiling hot tea onto your genitals.

8 **Sitting Down** – You're probably reading this sitting down, aren't you? Sitting is one of the most passive things you can do; it burns very few calories. From 9am to 6pm, five days a week – around 100,000-hours of your life – you are putting absolutely no strain on your body whatsoever.

9 **Snacking** – Most office employers snack at least two times a day more than those who work outdoors. Excessive snacking on sugar-rich treats – especially while sitting down – can increase your chances of obesity, diabetes and tooth decay.

10 **Stress** – One in three of us is constantly living with extreme stress, caused by work and money anxieties. Ironically, stressed workers are 10-20 per cent less productive than happy workers. Excessive stress can lead to heart attacks, psychological issues and death (see Karo-shi). Get out while you're still alive!

Please Wash
Your Hands

Sixty-three per cent of all your male co-workers won't have washed
their hands after going to the bathroom. Acceptable if it's a No.1,
a bit rude if it's a No.2.

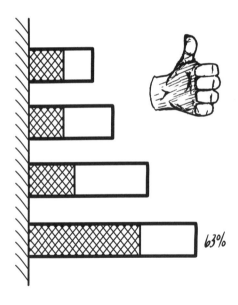

63%

Big Boss,
Little Compassion

Your boss, or manager, is no doubt a fountain of knowledge and industry expertise with decades of relevant experience. Below is a helpful guide to the ten things your boss knows about workplace compassion, however:

1.
2.
3.
4.
5.
6.
7.
8.
9.
10.

Be More Dutch

With Sweden trialling six-hour working days in 2015, it will be interesting to see what other countries reduce their working week hours in the wake of its impact. Let's hope that a three-day working week becomes the international standard by the year 2020.

1. **Netherlands:** 1,381 hours – **NICE!**

2. **Germany:** 1,397 hours

3. **Norway:** 1,420 hours

4. **France:** 1,479 hours

5. **Denmark:** 1,526 hours

6. **Ireland:** 1,529 hours

7. **Belgium:** 1,574 hours

8. **Luxembourg:** 1,609 hours

9. **Sweden:** 1,621 hours

10. **Slovenia:** 1,640 hours

11. **Switzerland:** 1,636 hours

12. **United States:** 1,654 hours

13. **Finland:** 1,672 hours

14. **Spain:** 1,686 hours

15. **Portugal:** 1,691 hours

16. **Austria:** 1,699 hours

17. Iceland: 1,706 hours

18. New Zealand: 1,706 hours

19. Canada: 1,710 hours

20. Australia: 1,728 hours

21 Japan: 1,746 hours

22. Italy: 1,752 hours

23. Slovak Republic: 1,785 hours,

24. United Kingdom: 1,790 hours

25. Czech Republic: 1,800 hours

26. Turkey: 1,855 hours

27. Hungary: 1,888 hours

28. Estonia: 1,889 hours

29. Israel: 1,910 hours

30. Poland: 1,929 hours

31. Russian Federation: 1,982 hours

32. Chile: 2,029 hours

33. Greece: 2,034 hours

34. Korea: 2,090 hours

35. Mexico: 2,226 hours – **NAUGHTY!**

Source (in case you thought we made it all up): Organisation for Economic Co-operation and Development (OECD)'s Better Life Index, 2015. Figures per year.

Office-Related Cocktails – Part 2

T.G.I.F.
It's Friday lunchtime... time to blow off some steam.

2 pints of lager, at lunchtime
1 glass of white wine, at lunchtime
1 shot of gin
½ as much work done as promised
1.30 train home

Monday Morning Blues
The perfect way to start a crap Monday...

3 shots of gin, mixed with
1 shot of vinegar (to disguise smell of booze)
1 breath mint (to disguise smell of vinegar)

Pay Rise Slammer

Forget the fact that you didn't get a pay rise this year. A Pay Rise Slammer will make you completely forget where you work:

2 shots of tequila
1 shot of vodka
1 shot Ouzo
1 snort of salt
1 lick of honey

Verbal Warning

Three Verbal Warnings and you're out!

2 shots of cognac
2 shots of bourbon
1 glass rim, sweetened with sugar

Day Off

The Day Off is everyone's favourite cocktail, designed to put everyone into a relaxed state of mind.

1 shot of milk
1 shot of dark rum
1 spoonful of honey
1 Valium

Office Dares –
Mind Games

Playing mind games on your colleagues is a hilarious way to inject some hilarity into the hours between 9 and 5, Monday to Friday. These mind games are best played out as "Long Cons" on the same person – can you keep them going the whole week?

1 Call the person you sit next to "Dan"

2 Write "Property of Dan" all over their office stationery

3 Change the clock to 12 minutes previous on your co-worker's computer everyday, before they arrive. By the end of the week, they would have lost a whole hour

4 Make constant tea rounds, three times a day, throughout the week. But always forget to make a drink for the same colleague each time, claiming, "Oh sorry, I forgot about you"

5 Tape a picture of your co-worker onto the underside lid of the photocopier. Every time someone makes a photocopy all that will be printed is his or her face

6 Watch them type their passcode into their smartphone, then when they leave the office without it, change the language settings of their phone to Danish. The look on their face when they return will be *uvurderlige*!

7 Set up a email account name juryselection@gov.uk, and email a co-worker telling them they have been selected for jury duty, starting tomorrow

8 Tell a co-worker that the photocopier is now voice-activated

9 Tell a co-worker they received a phone call, while they were away from their desk, from "someone calling himself the Judge", and that "you have broken a blood oath" and to "watch your back". Then tell them he didn't leave a number to call back on

Office Prank #13 – Keyboard Garden

When your colleague, or boss, goes away for an extended holiday, this is your chance to strike. Go to their desk and extract every letter key from the keyboard, one by one. Once that's done, fill in the holes with garden soil. Now, comes the fun bit. Plant some grass seed into the keyboard and ever-so-slightly water. Pat down the seeds. Shine their desktop lamp onto the keyboard and walk away whistling.

When your colleague arrives back to the office there should be a nice little green patch of newly grown garden lawn waiting for them as a welcome back present.

Shut The Front Door

Excessive swearing in offices is usually not tolerated, but it still happens every now and again when a notification email comes through requesting your presence at yet another unnecessary meeting.

So, instead of effing and blinding like a football hooligan, why not substitute your swearing by shouting this handy little ACRONYM below instead. Your boss will think you are beating yourself up trying to super proactive, but really you're telling everyone in the office precisely what you think of them. Remember, it's all about FOCUS.

FOCUS=

F**K

OFF

COS

UR

STUPID

Office Prank #17 –
Air Horn

Buy an air horn, plus air canister from the Internet. Get it delivered to work. Once it arrives, sellotape it under a co-worker's swivel chair. When they sit down, the noise will make their bowels turn to jelly. Priceless.

Hide And Sleep

Hide and Seek is a popular children's game. As you're an adult, and work in an office, why not play Hide and Sleep instead. The rules of the game are simple. Find a place in the office to hide. And sleep. The winner is the player who can't be found between the hours of 09:00 and 17:30.

Playlist About Hardly Working

Songs to chillax out to…

▸ 1. **I'm A Lazy Sod – Sex Pistols**

▸ 2. **The Life of Riley – The Lightning Seeds**

▸ 3. **I Don't Have to Be Me ('Til Monday) – Steve Azar**

▸ 4. **Beats Workin' – Van Halen**

▸ 5. **Lazy Bones – Green Day**

▸ 6. **I'm So Tired – The Beatles**

▸ 7. **Why Don't You Get A Job – The Offspring**

▸ 8. **Chillin Wiv Da Man Dem – Dizzee Rascal**

▸ 9. **I Need To Wake Up – Melissa Etheridge**

▸ 10. **Wake Me Up Before You Go Go – Wham!**

Alternatives To Swearing

Every office worker is complained about at least once in their career and encouraged to reduce their swearing so as not to offend other people's "delicate sensibilities". While most managers realize the importance of their employee's expressing themselves freely, it has become "corporate policy" at many international companies to try an innovative approach to swearing, using alternative phrases. The table below highlights some of the most commonly used examples:

INSTEAD OF	TRY SAYING
You don't know what the f**k you are doing	Do you know what you're doing?
She's a total, ball-busting mega bitch	She's an ambitious overachiever
When the f**k do you expect me to do this?	I'll work late then, I guess
No f**king way!	I believe that is unfair
You've got to be sh*tting me!	Really? How very odd
I don't give a sh*t!	That's someone else's problem
Not my f**k ing problem	Nothing to do with me
What the f**k?	That's interesting. Tell me more
This sh*t won't work	I'm not sure this is a valid request
Don't waste my f**k ing time	This will take longer than you expect
He's got his head up his arse	He's not aware of the issues
Eat sh*t, you idiot	Excuse me, what did you say?
Shove the job up your arse	I don't think you understand
This job sucks	I love a challenge
My boss has just f**k ed me in the arse	My boss is a pain in the bottom

Orwellian Tea

In 1946, the famed writer of the literary masterpiece 1984, George Orwell, wrote an essay about his 11 rules for making the perfect cup of tea. As an office worker you're used to following stupid rules – but how many of these do you actually follow?

"When I look through my own recipe for the perfect cup of tea I find no fewer than eleven outstanding points. Here are my own eleven rules, every one of which I regard as golden:"

1 Always use Indian tea. "the phrase 'a nice cup of tea' invariably means Indian tea."

2 Tea should be made in small quantities — that is, "in a teapot"

3 The pot should be warmed beforehand.

4 The tea should be strong. "I maintain that one strong cup of tea is better than twenty weak ones."

5 The tea should be poured straight into the pot.

6 Take the teapot to the kettle and not the other way about.

7 After making the tea, one should stir it, "or better, give the pot a good shake."

8 Drink out of a good breakfast cup.

9 You should pour the cream off the milk before using it for tea.

10 Pour tea into the cup. "By putting the tea in first and stirring as one pours, one can regulate the amount of milk."

Office Prank #14 –
Out Of Order

An oldie but a goodie. This is a classic office prank.

1) Print out a sheet of A4 with the words' "**OUT OF ORDER**" printed on it, in Comic Sans MS font, naturally.

2) Now, tape this sign to anything – toilet doors, printers, photocopiers, your bosses door, the ceiling – everything.

3) Watch the office descend into beautiful chaos.

Top 15 Movies That Are Set In The Workplace

Movies are a great way to suspend our disbelief, believe in magic, and escape from the dull monontony of our daily routines of office life. But, for some bizarre reason, we also love to watch movies that are set in offices. It's as if we can't get enough of punishing ourselves! If you haven't seen them, these classic movies are a must. Don't forget to watch them at work, for that added sense of reality...

1. **Office Space**
2. **Glengarry Glen Ross**
3. **Broadcast News**
4. **Nine to Five**
5. **The Intern**
6. **All The President's Men**
7. **Boiler Room**
8. **Working Girl**
9. **Wall Street**
10. **Horrible Bosses**
11. **The Apartment**
12. **The Devil Wears Prada**
13. **Up In The Air**
14. **In the Company of Men**
15. **The Internship**

Office One Liners

Sneak these witty one-liners in next time you need to sound clever at work...

1. A clean desk is a sign of a cluttered desk drawer.

2. If at first you don't succeed, redefine success.

3. A thing not worth doing isn't worth doing well.

4. If a thing is worth doing, it would have been done already.

5. The floggings will continue until morale improves.

6. I don't have a solution, but I do admire the problem.

7. Many people quit looking for work when they find a job.

8. Bureaucrats cut red tape, lengthwise.

9. Forty-three per cent of all statistics are made up.

10. A committee is a group of people who individually can do nothing, but as a group decide that nothing can be done.

Quote Quota #99

" I love deadlines. I like the whooshing sound they make as they fly by. "

Douglas Adams

Office Bantz #1

I thought I saw a light at the end of the tunnel, but it was only some moron with a torch bringing me more work.

Office-opoly

Bored? Of course you are. Why not create your own Office version of the popular board game Monopoly then? Print your own money, devise your own board rules, and use items such as paperclips, and pen-tops as player pieces. Collect £200 every time you pass Go, and don't stop until everyone has bought hotels on delux office space, or is completely broke. The longer the game the better – why not see if you can keep a game going for a whole week?

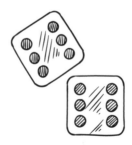

Office Prank #15 – Advertise Your Next Meeting

Photocopy this sign, below, and pin it to the company noticeboard.

ARE YOU LONELY?

Tired of working on your own?
Do you hate making decisions?

COME TO MY NEXT MEETING!

Together we can feel important, eat biscuits, use the projector, be impressed with our PowerPoint skills, and disguise wasting our time as genuine work!

*Go To Meeting Room A – **NOW!***

Evil Companies In Movies

Your company may be unethical, tyrannical and employ incompetent micro-managers, but just be thankful it's not quite as bad as these guys:

1. **Weyland-Utani Corporation,** *Aliens*
2. **Umbrella Corporation,** *Resident Evil*
3. **InGen Inc.,** *Jurassic Park*
4. **Multi-National United (MNU),** *District 9*
5. **Tyrell Corporation,** *Blade Runner*
6. **Engulf and Devour Corporation,** *Silent Movie*
7. **Cyberdyne Systems,** *Terminator 2: Judgment Day*
8. **Initech,** *Office Space*
9. **Soylent Corporation,** *Soylent Green*
10. **RDA Corporation,** *Avatar*

Quote Quota #44

> **Work is just another of man's diseases and prevention is better than the cure. If you don't look for work, work won't look for you.**
>
> Heathcote Williams

Office Bantz #2

A popular office joke for you...

"This is the story about four people named Everybody, Somebody, Anybody, and Nobody. There was an important job to be done and Everybody was sure that Somebody would do it. Anybody could have done it, but nobody did it. Somebody got angry about that, because it was Everybody's job. Everybody thought that anybody could do it, but Nobody realized that Everybody wouldn't do it. It ended up that Everybody blamed Somebody, when Nobody did what Anybody could of done."

In Case Of Emergency

This useful destress kit, below, will help keep you on the right side of sanity. Use only once.

1. **Place this page on a firm surface. Feel free to tear out.**
2. **Follow directions in circle below**
3. **Repeat until you are de-stressed or become unconscious**

**BANG
HEAD
HERE**

Rise Of The Zombie

Lately, it seems like every time we turn on the TV, or surf the Internet there is a new zombie-related TV show or movie. It's as if TV executives who commission this sh*t know that we are lifeless zombies ourselves, thanks to our robot-drone roles at brain-chewing corporations that are quite literally sucking the life out of us – and we swallow it up like the sheep we are.

1. *iZombie*

2. *Zombieland*

3. *Z Nation*

4. *The Walking Dead*

5. *Fear The Walking Dead*

6. *World War Z*

7. *Shaun Of The Dead*

8. *Dead Set*

9. *Warm Bodies*

10. *The Returned*

Reasons We Hate Going To Work, Part 3

...And on...

1 People who eat salads for lunch

2 People who cycle to work

3 People who go for lunchtime runs

4 People who eat healthy snacks

5 Co-workers who never make tea or coffee for anyone except themselves

6 Work appraisals

7 Colleagues who tell you how stressed they are – all the time

8 Working to a deadline with a hangover

9 Time passing ridiculously slowly

10 Introducing yourself to the New Guy

Motivational Work Slogans

Some companies hang motivational slogans around the office. They're there to make you work harder. Feel free to print these ones off – and then graffiti them with penis doodles.

Dreams don't work unless you do

ALL ROADS THAT LEAD TO SUCCESS HAVE TO PASS THROUGH HARD WORK BOULEVARD AT SOME POINT

If you want to make something for yourself, work harder than everybody else

Imagine. Believe. Achieve.

Winners are not people who never fail, but people who never quit

Every day may not be good, but there is something good in every day

ATTITUDE IS EVERYTHING

Every accomplishment starts with the decision to try

Work harder than you think you did yesterday

KEEP CALM AND CARRY ON

Job Title Generator

The office is the only workplace in the world where you are legally allowed – nay, it's your duty – to sex up your boring job title into something a lot more dazzling for your CV. To your disappointed parents you may just be a desk donkey and wave slave, but for perspective employers why not add a bit more dazzle to your boring daily roles?

1   **Data entry**   Computer Remuneration Assistant

2   **Answering the telephone**   Telecommunication Executive

3   **Dish Washer**   Crockery Cleansing Operative

4   **Post-room worker**   Dispatch Services Facilitator

5   **Tidying the office**   Environment Improvement Technician

6   **Filling in for Reception**   Frontline Customer Liaison

7 **Lifting boxes**   Resource Operative

8 **Putting the bins out**   Waste management and Disposal Technician

9 **Making the tea**   Refreshment Coordinator

10 **Filing**   Storage Assistant

11 **Photocopying stuff**   File Duplication Assistant

12 **Setting up invoices**   Payment Facilitator

How To Make The Perfect Paper Aeroplane

A decade ago, with the advent of the Internet, emails and hard drives, we all thought that by the year 2015, we'd be commuting to work on our hoverboards and working in "paperless offices". Alas, neither of those things has come true. We still waste as much pristine, pure-as snow, gleaming white 100gsm A4 paper as we have ever used. While most of us are spectacularly environment-conscious, there are a few dinosaurs in the office who still print documents out like there is no tomorrow, simply because they find it easier to read than on the screen.

To counterbalance these morons, let's put their waste to good use. Any time you see printed pieces of A4 paper going to waste, don't just put it straight in the recycling bin. It is your environmental duty to have a bit of fun with it first.

Here's how:

Here are our easy step-by-step instructions. For hilarious results, use paper that has swear words printed all over one side.

 Non-sweary side up. Fold the page in half along Line 1.

 Open the paper up again. Fold down corners towards you so that they meet at the centre fold.

3

Now fold the triangle made by A & B down the non-sweary side.

4

Take corners C and D and fold them in towards the centre of the page until their points touch E and F respectively.

5

This is what you should have so far– the sweary side is now showing.

6

Now fold up the little triangle marked "FLAP" so that it covers (and "locks" corners C & D.

7

Fold the paper back in half along down the centre line.

8

Now fold down the "wings" along so that the two halves of the plane meet.

How To Win At Office Politics

If you're determined to make the most out of your time between 9 and 5, then follow these 20 golden rules to office politicking, below:

1 Play the game/play the long game

2 Form alliances, gather an army

3 Take all the credit, even when there is none to take

4 Manipulate the weak, eradicate the gullible

5 Show favouritism and play favourites

6 Flatter everyone, adore no one

7 Schmooze and network at every opportunity

8 Learn to read people's tells

9 Admit your mistakes, before others point them out

10 Backstab those in your way

11 Spread false rumours

12 Scheme and lie to get what you want

13 Never accept "no", never say "no"

14 Choose your battles

15 Spend time and befriend senior staff outside of work

16 Keep a paper trail / Remember other people's mistakes

17 Don't get embroiled in petty fights

18 Never appear to have a personal life

19 Appear humble to those who can help you

20 Keep a positive mental attitude at all times

The Importance Of Being Idle, Part 1

Getting bored – it'll happen at least ten times a day. So here's a handy little To Do list for when boredom creeps into you mind and strangles your thoughts.

1 Write a list of all things you'd buy if you had £10 million in the bank

2 Write a chronological list of everyone you've ever kissed and slept with

3 Write a Pros and Cons list about your partner

4 Write your Christmas Cards, even if it's March

5 Write a handwritten letter to an elderly relative

6 Write a will and testament

7 Write a list of all the people you hate and what they did to piss you off

8 Rank all your friends in order of preference

9 Write a Pros and Cons list about yourself. Email it to your partner

10 Create an alter ego. Then create an online dating profile

Quote Quota #89

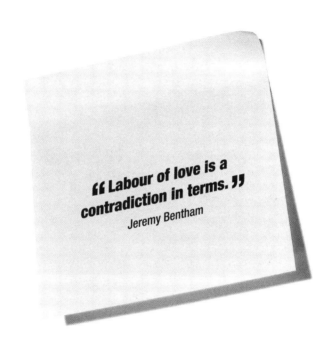

❝ Labour of love is a contradiction in terms. ❞
Jeremy Bentham

Office Dares #19 – Write A Theme Tune For The Office

No office is complete without a theme tune. Spend the day writing lyrics about your fellow colleagues, download Garageband app (or any music software available) onto your smartphone and compose a jaunty upbeat melody – or macabre downbeat ballad – that perfectly sums up life in your office. Here are some sample lyrics, to help you on your way…

This is our office
it's a place where things are neat
And Jenny in accounts,
with boobs that always bounce,
makes going upstairs
such a treat

There's lovely Dan in marketing
in fact there's two
there's always a guy called Dan
in every office
and that's just the truth

The boss is a meathead
who hasn't a clue
got a degree in Leisure Management
in 2002
Everyone hates him
for everything that he says
his LinkedIn picture profile
makes him look like a frog

And so on...

Worst Personality Types In An Office

The worst – and I mean *the worst* – thing about working in an office is not that these personality types exist in an office, but the fact that no matter how hard you try, your colleagues have definitely got you tagged as at least one of them. So, which is it?

1 The micromanager

2 The workaholic

3 The kiss-ass

4 The stresshead

5 The cool guy

6 The boss's son/daughter

7 The office gossip

8 Mr Motivated

9 The super-ambitious

10 The egomaniac

11 The nice but dim

12 The panicker

13 The wisecracker

14 The person with the annoying laugh

15 The person you wouldn't trust further than you could throw them

All Up In Your Business

Backstabbing your co-workers, so that they never get promoted above you, is easy to do in an office. And fun! There's no "I" in team, remember. Here's how to do it:

1 Keep a tally of who comes in late every day, then anonymously email the list to your manager

2 Spread a rumour alleging that that person to whom you are spreading the rumour is disliked by another employee

3 Agree with everything they say publically, but denounce their ideas when in private with their manager

4 When the need to fart comes up, walk over to their desk, drop the bomb, then leave. Then complain about the smell from the other side of the room

5 Invite everyone else to lunch and work drinks, except one person. Rotate who that person is, so that you can gossip about everyone, but no one can gossip about you

6 Get everyone to endorse you publicly on LinkedIn. And then never repay the favour

7 When co-workers go on vacation, orchestrate a campaign of hate towards them and their work.

8 Take credit for other people's ideas when they are not in the room, but only give yourself credit for the "initial idea ... everything else was up to them"

Commuter Hell

Look out for these other office drones who will get in your way on your way to the office:

1 Those who get on, and then shout "Move down", on already crushed train carriages.

2 Those who roll their eyes and make that "tsk" noise when someone shouts "move down" at them.

3 Lycra louts on bikes who think they're Lance Armstrong and smugly think the roads belong to them

4 People whose hot breath you can feel on your neck

5 People who jam the doors of Underground carriages and make the rest of us late

6 Train drivers with a cheery disposition

7 Bus drivers who don't stop even though the bus isn't full

8 People who listen to music on their smartphones but don't wear headphones

9 People who look over your shoulder when you're sending a text

10 People who look elderly berate you when you give up your seat for them, when actually they're not that old, and they don't need to sit down

Office Dare #21 – Sellotape Selfie

Find some Sellotape. Wrap it around your head. Make sure your forehead is stretched back, your hair is sticking up, your eyes are bulbous, your nose is squashed, your mouth is mangled and your tongue is out. Take a selfie. Email to everyone at work and ask him or her to beat it. The selfie that looks the most demented wins a prize.

Google Map It

In your darkest, most bored moments, be honest you love nothing more than Google mapping your own house in street view. Well, let's take this idea one step further. Let's look up the world's funniest place names and have a sniff around in street view.

1. **Intercourse,** Pennsylvania, USA
2. **F*cking,** Austria
3. **Hell,** Norway
4. **Dildo,** Canada
5. **Twatt,** Scotland
6. **Middelfart,** Denmark
7. **Muff,** Ireland
8. **Titty Hill Farm,** UK
9. **Anus,** France
10. **Bastardo,** Perugia, Italy

How To Get The Sack, Part 1

Getting fired isn't as easy as you think. You've got to really think outside the box these days if you want to get the sack. Which is ironic, isn't it?

1 Sell office supplies and stationery on eBay

2 Burn CDs of movies you've downloaded illegally at work (using work DVD-Rs) and sell them to your colleagues

3 Leave the office every day with your bag packed with toilet rolls, teabags, A4 paper, laptops – anything you can sell at a Car Boot Sale

4 Request that people only refer to you as "Super"

5 Start wearing the exact same clothes as your boss, and copy everything he does

6 Buy a new kitchen, on expenses

7 Pretend to throw up in your mouth every time you hear corporate jargon

8 Organize meetings and then never show up

9 Send your boss selfies of you at a theme park, or in a pub, after you called in "sick"

10 Show up to work every other weekday

11 Start bringing a dog to work – it can be a different dog every day

12 Start growing marijuana on your desk. This becomes apparent only when the plant is in full bloom

Quote Quota #128

" What I don't like about office Christmas parties is looking for a job the next day. "

Phyllis Diller

How To Get The Sack, Part 2 – Live Tweet Your Day

Social media is ruining all our lives one tweet at a time, but it can sometimes come in handy. If you want to get sacked from your sh*tty office job, then this is the quickest and easiest way. Start tweeting your own company's Twitter account with live tweets about how little you are accomplishing that day. Here are a few examples to get you started:

Arrived late this morning. Thinking about watching The Godfather in the toilet before starting any work. Love my job!
@company

Boss is away today. The mice will play. Three-hour lunch! #boozeup
@company

*This place is soooooooooo sh*t!*
@company

Biggest. Poo. Ever. #floater*
@company

*include photo attachment

How To Survive An Office Job

If it's your first day in an office, don't panic, just remember these guidelines and you'll be just fine...

1. **Nothing really matters**

2. **Nobody really cares**

3. **What's the worst that could happen?**

4. **There's always tomorrow**

5. **Everybody makes mistakes**

6. **At the end of the day, nobody died**

7. **Always look on the bright side**

8. **It's just a job**

9. **There's a 1 per cent chance you could die in your sleep**

10. **Rome wasn't built in a day**

How To Poo At Work

If you work in an office where toilet cubicles are at a premium right after breakfast and directly after lunch, and you don't want people to hear your plopping, splashing and grunting, then don't worry, this is how to avoid the embarrassment:

1 Eat out of sync with everyone else – that way, your bowel movement schedule will not align with anyone else's.

2 Always use a toilet on a different floor. That way, co-workers won't know that you're the one in there making all the noise.

3 Every office has a secret bathroom. Find it. Use it. Keep quiet about it..

4 Tell your colleagues you're in a "meeting room making a call", then pop to the loo. Nobody will be suspicious of your absence and nobody will notice when you stroll back in 45 minutes later.

5 Try to minimize your poo-ing to under ten minutes. Unless your book is really good.

6 Lay a few pieces of toilet roll in the waterbowl. This will suppress the sound of the poo hitting the water like a bomb. It acts like a silencer on a gun. Sort of.

7 Have an escape plan ready. Know which exit to use. Don't go to the sink with the empty soap dispenser. Remember always be poo-prepared.

8 Buy some fake legs from Amazon. Put them in the stalls opposite you. When people walk in, they'll see all the stalls are occupied and leave you in peace.

9 Go to a nearby restaurant and poo there.

10 Be proud of your poo. Be confident of your grunting, and let your poo plop with panache. Don't be afraid to poo if there's someone in the other cubicle. If anyone looks horrified at you, just tell him or her, "it's a part of life – GET OVER IT", and storm out. After washing your hands, of course.

*Is Your Job Bullsh*t?*

The obvious answer is clearly yes. But in order to waste a few hours and to complete your due diligence (which you don't apply in your day job), take this quiz below, and find out for sure.

1 Could someone without any qualifications do your job? ☐

2 Could your role be carried out if you weren't present in the building? ☐

3 Could your work be outsourced to an automated robot of some sort? ☐

4 Do you do anything that actually changes your company in any way? ☐

5 If yes, do you see those changes on a day-to-day basis? ☐

6 If your job wasn't done daily, do you believe that the company would be unable to function? ☐

7 Could a monkey, with no experience of language or cognitive function, be able to complete the tasks you do? ☐

8 Do you attend meetings where the outcome alters the company's working method or profits in any way? ☐

9 Do you feel like you're working towards a realistically achievable goal that will make the world a better place? ☐

10 If your job didn't exist, would anyone think to create it? ☐

11 Did your job exist 50 years ago? ☐

12 Is your company's success dependent on you turning up for work? ☐

13 Do you think a machine would do your job more accurately? ☐

14 Are you currently experiencing redundancies at your workplace and throughout your industry in roles similar to yours? ☐

If you answered every question, congratulations, you wasted some time! Who cares about the answers? Your job is bullsh*t. Take comfort in the fact you knew that anyway.

Six Tips To Calling In "Sick" And Getting Away With It

Pulling a sickie can often make you genuinely ill, due to the anxiety and bowel-trembling fear you experience waiting to make that call to your boss. Will they believe you? Here's some handy tips to make sure they do…

1 Make the call at 9.01am – be proactive about it. Don't put it off

2 Don't leave a voicemail – call back every five minutes until you speak to your boss personally

3 Be confident and to the point – don't bumble on for ten minutes apologizing

4 No fake ill sounds and weak coughs – remember you have to go back to work tomorrow, you can't be too ill

5 Ask if there is anything you can do remotely from home, if you "find the strength"

6 Apologize once and only once. Remember you've got nothing to apologize for – you can't help being "ill", right?

Quote Quota #37

❝ If something's worth doing, it's worth doing rihgt ❞

Peter Serafinowicz

Top Ten Excuses _Not_ To Use When Calling In Sick*

*These were genuine excuses some employees gave to their employers in 2012/2013, according to a survey of 1,000 workers and 1,000 employees. Shocking!

1 A can of baked beans landed on my big toe

2 I was swimming too fast and smacked my head on the poolside

3 I've been bitten by an insect

4 My car handbrake broke and it rolled down the hill into a lamppost

5 My dog has had a big fright and I don't want to leave him

6 My hamster died

7 I've injured myself during sex

8 I've had a sleepless night

9 My mum has died (this was the second time the person used this excuse

10 I am hallucinating

11 I am stuck in my house because the door is broken

12 My new girlfriend bit me in a delicate place

13 I burned my hand on the toaster

14 The dog ate my shoes

15 My fish is sick

16 I swallowed white spirit

17 My toe is trapped in the bath tap

18 I'm in A&E, as I got a clothes peg stuck on my tongue

19 I drank too much and fell asleep on someone's floor – I don't know where I am

20 My trousers split on the way to work

Words To Make You Sound Clever

Drop these smart bombs into conversations, and your boss may just *not* look at you with contempt today. Not a guarantee.

1 **Byzantine**   Highly involved or intricate

2 **Capricious**   Impulsive and unpredictable

3 **Dilettante**   Showing frivolous or superficial interest

4 **Equanimity**   Steadiness of mind under stress

5 **Fastidious**   Difficult to please

6 **Finagle**   To trick, swindle or cheat

7 **Machiavellian**   Unprincipled and crafty

8   **Philistine**   A person who is uninterested in intellectual pursuits

9   **Quid pro quo**   This for that

10   **Sycophant**   A self-serving flatterer, a brownnoser

11   **Ubiquitous**   Being present everywhere at once

12   **Zealous**   Enthusiastic; fervent; fanatical

13   **Boondoggle**   Work of little or no value done merely to look busy

14   **Malinger**   To evade responsibility by pretending to be ill

It's A Dirty Job But Someone's Got To Do It...

Working in an office is so dreadful that 8 out of ten people still would prefer to work at the jobs below than work inside an office.

1 Portable Toilet Cleaner

2 Sewage Treatment Workers

3 Toilet Attendant

4 Nude Model

5 Embalmer

6 Roadkill Collector

7 Castrato

8 Poultry Kill Room Attendant

9 Animal Masturbator

10 Pet Food Taster

11 Sewer Inspector

12 Baby Chicken Sexer

Piles Of Work

There are lots of strains and pressures we put on our body during our average week at the office. Not least on our poor behinds, which get sat on for hours on end with little exercise in between. Below is a list of famous people who suffered from piles – perhaps they also spent too much time on the loo, hiding from work and their bosses.

1. **Alfred the Great**
2. **Napoleon Bonaparte**
3. **Ernest Hemingway**
4. **Marilyn Monroe**
5. **Karl Marx**
6. **Elizabeth Taylor**

Get Awkward #2

Grab your boss' hand on your walk to the next staff meeting. If they try to let go – which they will – simply tell them, "Sorry, I must have misread the situation," before mouthing the words "I love you" to them as they walk into the meeting room. This will completely discombobulate them for the entire meeting.

FYI #3

The average commute to work, in the UK, takes 45 minutes and the average distance travelled is approximately 8½ miles. That's at least a 16-mile round trip every day. However, recent studies show that office fingers will travel 2.6 miles across the keyboard every single day!

Me Time

Spending time in cramped workspaces, cubicles and "desk stations" with people we resent and ridicule is tough work. Every now and then you need a little ME TIME in the office, which isn't just sat down on the loo watching Netflix and occasionally flushing to let people know you haven't disappeared down the hole. Here are some great ways to enjoy some quality ME TIME at work:

1 **Book a Meeting Room** – and then just hide there for hours pretending to work.

2 **Walk "to the Post Office"** – pretend you have something important to send.

3 **Listen to a "work-related podcast" on your iPhone** – it's actually Beyoncé's latest album.

4 **Watch a "TED Talk" with your headphones in** – no one will realize it has nothing to do with your job.

5 **Make a tea round** – for the whole office. Gets you away from your desk for a good 20 minutes.

Up In Your Business

The average person – that's you – spends 100,000 hours of their 650,000 hours alive on earth life pursuing a career. if you work in an office, that's 100,000 hours of smelling other people's farts and BO.

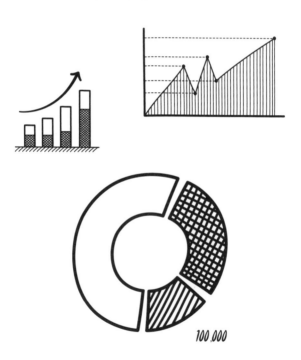

100,000

Quote Quota #21

❝And on the seventh day God ended his work which he had made and he rested on the seventh day from all his work which he had made.❞

Genesis II, Verse II

Famous People Who Lost Their Jobs Before They Were Famous

Lord Sugar is famous for pointing at hapless individuals and telling them, "You're Fired", to the nation's squeals of delight. But, in truth, getting fired is one of the most embarrassing things that can happen to an office worker. Thankfully, job loss has happened to these wonderful people too...

1 Walt Disney (he "lacked imagination and had no good ideas")

2 J.K. Rowling (got the boot as a secretary from Amnesty International)

3 Anna Wintour ("I recommend that you all get fired," she said after)

4 Madonna (she was let go on her first day after squirting jelly on her customers)

5 Oprah Winfrey (as a news anchor for Baltimore's WJZ-TV)

6 Robert Redford (was found asleep on the job!)

7 Thomas Edison (spilled acid on the floor of a laboratory)

8 Steve Jobs (fired from Apple, the company he created)

9 Michael Jordan (was cut from his high school basketball team!)

10 Rudyard Kipling ("You just don't know how to use the English language," his newspaper editor told him)

Top Ten Ways To Avoid Fixing A Printer Jam

All sorts of things go wrong in an office – on a daily basis. But when a printer breaks down, so does the humanity of your colleagues. Here's how to avoid doing what they won't.

1. **Pretend to go to a meeting –
   let someone else notice and fix it.**
2.
3.
4.
5.
6.
7.
8.
9.
10. **Hopefully by now, it's fixed.**

PRINTER JAM RULES
If it's broke, don't try to fix it.
If you broke it, don't try to fix it.
If someone else broke it, let everyone know you didn't break it.

110%

Are you always told to "do more" at work? Do you always give 110 per cent? No?

Well, here's our guaranteed guide to always giving 110 per cent at work. If anyone ever doubts your work ethic – and they should – throw these percentages about how hard you work back in their face.

Monday 30 per cent
Tuesday 30 per cent
Wednesday 25 per cent
Thursday 23 per cent
Friday 2 per cent

Total = 110 per cent

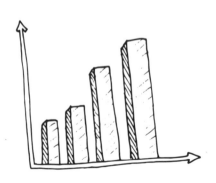

Mr Jobs

You can't have a book about office jobs and not talk about the man whose inventions have saved us all from actually doing our job – the late, great Steve Jobs (1955–2011). Thanks to this man's efforts, we now have the weapons of mass distraction to help us achieve less at work as well as stop us from getting bored. His achievements can be listed quite simply – just randomly put an "i" in front of any word and you'll probably name many of Apple's bestselling products. But here are definitely ten of his best creations, in no particular order.

1 **Apple Music** (great to listen to drown out colleagues voices)

2 **Apple Music Festival** (a place to go to that isn't work)

3 **iPhone** (to distract you from all work that needs to be done)

4 **Pixar Animation Studios** (great movies to watch when the boss is out)

5 **iMac** (beats using a fax)

6 **iPad** (pocket-sized – perfect for hiding on your desk)

7 **iPod** (once a great way to smuggle music into work hours)

8 **The App Store** (Angry Birds – great for toilet breaks)

9 **Apple Store** (a great place to work, should you be made redundant)

10 **Bringing back black polo neck jumpers into fashion** (they've always suited you)

Top Ten: How To Get Ahead In Business

Work may be nine hours of boredom punctuated by a few random minutes of fear, anxiety and panic, but for those of you who actually want to succeed at work (without really trying), then this list below is guaranteed to help you along the way:

1 Always leave one minute after the boss has gone, never before

2 Make sure your tea mug is the mug with the company logo on

3 Decorate your workspace with motivational signs and quotations; print off new quotations every week and place them near your monitor

4 Routinely send round all-staff emails alerting colleagues to sponsor your most recent charity crowd-funding event

5 Always walk round the office holding folders, and always look as if you're in a rush to get to wherever it is you're going – even if it's just the toilet

6 Every time you see your boss, compliment them on their hair, clothes or appearance. Drip-fed flattery goes a long way

7 Bring in baked treats, chocolates and sweets at least twice a week

8 Never call in sick: it's better to fake an illness and then be sent home rather than have colleagues question your illness when you're not there

9 Keep a journal of every unflattering or gossipy utterance that a co-worker says about another co-worker, or every time your boss does something fraudulent or illegal in terms of company policy. This journal might one day save your life

10 Develop really unreadable handwriting and then appear to take copious amounts of "important" notes in every meeting you ever attend. Even if you're just scribbling down the word "tits" over and over again, co-workers will think you're being attentive and officious

Inbox Full

It is estimated that 144.8 billion emails are sent ever single day. That's around 20 emails per person for every man, woman and child on earth! Sixty-five per cent of all those emails sent are spam and 30 per cent of all your emails sent during working hours are personal. The average office worker spends 36 days a year answering work emails. Office workers in London, in particular, receive close to 9,000 emails each year – roughly 25 emails a day.

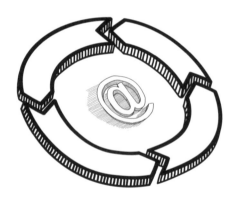

Playlist – Songs To Calm You Down

Stressful meeting? Frustrating appraisal? We feel your pain. This playlist will help lower your blood pressure...

▶ 1. **Queen – Don't Stop Me Now**

▶ 2. **Fleetwood Mac – Go Your Own Way**

▶ 3. **Snow Patrol – Chasing Cars**

▶ 4. **The Black Eyed Peas – Let's Get It Started**

▶ 5. **Coldplay – Paradise**

▶ 6. **Lily Allen – Smile**

▶ 7. **Prince – Purple Rain**

▶ 8. **Tracy Chapman – Fast Car**

▶ 9. **Calvin Harris – Ready for the Weekend**

▶ 10. **George Ezra – Budapest**

Quote Quota #12

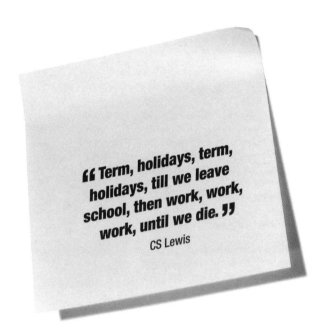

" Term, holidays, term, holidays, till we leave school, then work, work, work, until we die. "

CS Lewis

Office Puns (We Love To Hate)

Try and sneak these crafty little puns into conversation, if only to make yourself laugh. Watch your co-workers' eyes roll with pain every time you whip them out:

To the Cleaner…
**Did you hear about the new broom that just came out?
It's sweeping the nation.**

To A Co-Worker
I ate a clock this morning and thought that was time consuming… but that meeting went on for hours.

To A Minion
**I just ate way too much Greek food for lunch.
Now I falafel.**

To the IT Manager
**If you don't fix Microsoft Office, you'll be in big trouble.
You have my Word.**

To your Boss
**I'm so committed to my job that I only eat office supplies.
It's a staple diet.**

To A Co-Worker
**Everyone's off work at the moment sick.
It must be a staff infection.**

Drawing A Blank

Focus all your boredom onto the blank square below. Don't stop until you feel all of the day's pointlessness and frustration running towards the exit door in your brain. Once you've finished, shake the book vigorously to waft away the negative energy you have absorbed throughout the day.

LOOK HERE!

The Never-To-Say And Never-To-Do List

Your bosses will spend much of their time wanting you to do what they say, but will never actually want you to say what they do. Because most of what they say is utter rubbish. Keep an ear out for these braincell-killing words of wisdom today....

1. **Push the envelope**

2. **Enjoy a thought shower**

3. **Kick the can around the garage**

4. **Press play on an idea**

5. **Brain storm**

6. **Make a reality sandwich**

7. **High-five a colleague after an excellent PowerPoint presentation**

8. **Ideagasm**

9. **Synergize**

10. **Trend upwards**

REMEMBER

Every time you hear these phrases, you lose 300 brain cells. How many more can you stand to lose?

Office Photocopier Rules

If the photocopier toner needs replacing or a paper jam occurs while you're using it, and to ensure the ongoing inefficient running of the office, please carry out the follow instructions:

1. **Walk away**
2. **Whistle a jaunty tune**
3. **Take an early lunch**

Get Awkward #3

Say the words "I love you" at the end of every conversation today.

" Kill my boss?
Do I dare live out the
American dream? "
Homer Simpson

Playlist – Songs To Get You Pumped Up To Ask For A Raise

Money makes the office go round, but yet the buck stops literally just before knocking at your door. Go figure. Pump yourself up into a frenzy and walk straight into your boss's office and don't take no for answer.

- ▶ 1. **Money For Nothing – Dire Straits**

- ▶ 2. **Working Day and Night – Michael Jackson**

- ▶ 3. **Take the Money and Run – The Steve Miller Band**

- ▶ 4. **Slave To The Wage – Placebo**

- ▶ 5. **I Need A Dollar – Aloe Blacc**

- ▶ 6. **After Taxes – Johnny Cash**

- ▶ 7. **Bills, Bills, Bills – Destiny's Child**

- ▶ 8. **Money, Money, Money – ABBA**

- ▶ 9. **Ka-Ching! – Shania Twain**

- ▶ 10. **Money – Pink Floyd**

Quote Quota #33

❝ Often, people work long hard hours at jobs they hate, to earn money to buy things they don't need, to impress people they don't like. ❞

Nigel Marsh

Post-it Note Prank

This is an oldie, but a goldie, and a prank that will provide a definite flash of colour and excitement to your dull, cold and lifeless working environment.

First things first: go to the stationery cupboard. I assume you know where this is. Pick up a six-pack of the large, squared Post-it notes. Any colour will suffice.

Next time your office nemesis – or just any old random work person who you can't stand the sight of – goes for lunch, quickly cover every square inch of their desk area with Post-its. Do not leave a space un-noted. Cover as much surface area as you can; there are 100 notes per pad, so you should be able to use up 600 Post-it notes without much effort. If you're worried about wasting good quality office supplies, then feel free to print out a whole ream of paper with pictures of David Hasselhoff in just his red *Baywatch* shorts instead, and decorate your victim's "working space" with more Hasselhoff chest hair than any one person should see in a lifetime.

Top Ten: Stressbusters

Forgot those squidgy little balls you crush between your palms. That's too easy. When you really need to bust some serious stress, try the following:

1 Try breaking a plastic 30cm ruler in half with your head (it's impossible)

2 Open up a Microsoft Word. doc and type as many different swear words as possible. Don't stop until you've drawn a complete blank. By then, your stress will have drained totally from your being and you will have gained a massive insight into your own devious psyche

3 Smell fresh coffee. This cheers everyone up

4 Rip a whole ream of A4 paper in half – good luck!

5 Google "Cat strokes pig" and watch the video that appears on repeat

6 Squirt a lemon in your eye or rub chilli in your eye – the pain will distract you from the stress

7 Staple your two perlicules together (Google what they are first)

8 Wrap a whole dispenser of sellotape around your head and then slowly untangle it – the pain will distract you from the stress

9 Edit a Wikipedia page

10 Write a list of everyone you've slept with – not in chronological order, but alphabetical

Things We'd All Like To Say To Our Boss

Most of us usually think of the perfect response to our manager's inane questions only after they've stormed out of the room. Have these lines prepared in advance and you'll always get the first and last word in…

"Of course I don't look busy. I did it right the first time."

"You've changed your mind? Well, there's a surprise."

"No, I'm not busy – feel free to waste my time."

"Would you like to offer to make me a cup of tea for once?"

"I'll stay late – if you do."

"The best part of my day is when you've stopped telling me how to do your job and concentrate on yours."

"You don't be mad to work here … but you definitely fulfil that criteria."

"I'm sorry I'm late, but I'd thought I'd be a bit more like you today."

"Good morning... well, it was before you arrived."

"Don't have a good night."

Quote Quota #91

❝ The brain is a wonderful organ. It starts working the moment you get up in the morning, and does not stop until you get into the office. ❞

Robert Frost

Office Monkeys

This is an old office joke, one you've probably heard a million times, but it's worth repeating because it accurately describes every office.

"An office is like a tree full of monkeys, all on different branches at different levels. The monkeys on top look down and see a tree full of smiling faces. The monkeys on the bottom look up and see nothing but arseholes."

Don't Walk, Snudge

Did you know there is an actual word to describe striding around the office trying to look terribly busy, when in fact you're doing nothing at all (except killing time). It's called snudging, from the verb to snudge. Give it a whirl – it might be the only thing that impresses your boss today!

Get Awkward #5

Place a segment of orange in the bottom of your mouth, a la Marlon Brando in The Godfather. Then send an email to your co-workers with the subject line: "An Offer You Can't Refuse". Anyone who comes to your desk to enquire what on earth you mean, tell them that you'll do whatever they ask of you for the rest of the day, while speaking in a heavy Italian-American accent like Don Corleone.

Dream Job

In October 2015, a survey from the *Independent* newspaper threw a spotlight on Britain's Ten Dream Jobs. Surprise, surprise! Not one of them is office-based. In fact, judging by the list, the entire country would rather be *absolutely anywhere else* than sitting at their desk in an office.

1. **Footballer**
2. **Private Detective**
3. **Actor**
4. **Spy**
5. **Becoming My Own Boss**
6. **Singer**
7. **Vet**
8. **Astronaut**
9. **Dancer**
10. **Mad Scientist**

Christmas Party Ingredients

Most office Christmas parties are a recipe for disaster. Here are all the ingredients you need to make this year's party as "unforgettable" as last year's:

Two office hunks
Three drunken chairman
Four accounting birds
No wedding rings
Six CEOs flirting
Seven interns crying
Eight empty stomachs
Nine sales assistants dancing
Ten salesman ogling
Eleven people puking
Twelve Uber bookings
and
A trip to the local A&E

Playlist – Songs To Start An Office Revolution

Revolt! Revolt! Turn these songs up loud now!

▶ 1. **Packt Like Sardines In A Crushd Tin Box – Radiohead**

▶ 2. **Bye Bye Bad Man – The Stone Roses**

▶ 3. **Everybody Wants To Rule The World – Tears For Fears**

▶ 4. **World Of Our Own – Westlife**

▶ 5. **I Want To Break Free – Queen**

▶ 6. **Revolution Song – Noel Gallagher**

▶ 7. **The Boy In the Bubble – Paul Simon**

▶ 8. **Drag Me Down – One Direction**

▶ 9. **Killing In The Name – Rage Against the Machine**

▶ 10. **I Hate My Job – Cam'ron**

Quote Quota #40

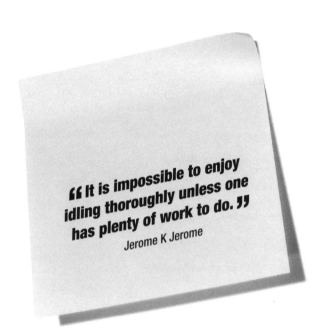

❝ It is impossible to enjoy idling thoroughly unless one has plenty of work to do. ❞

Jerome K Jerome

Working Day Breakdown

We constantly moan to our co-workers how much work we have on but, let's be honest, no matter how busy we claim to be, we still spend most of day trying hard not to work. Like so:

09:00–09:15 Arrival time

09:15–09:45 Breakfast

09:45–10:00 Toilet

10:15–11:00 Check your inbox, reply to personal emails

11:00–11:30 Make your round of tea; cruise the office to see what people are doing for lunch

11:30–12:00 Check Facebook/Twitter/Instagram

12:00–12:30 Prepare for lunch

12:30–13:45 Lunch

13:45–14:00 Toilet

14:00–14:15 Make another round of tea

14:15–15.30 A pointless meeting

15:30–16:00 Confirm plans for the evening with friends/partner/family

16:00–16:45 General web browsing

16:45–17:15 Urgently cram in all the work for the day

17:15–17:25 Prepare to go home

17:28 Go home

Total work time: 2.5 hours

Total time wasted: 5.5 hours

Germ-Infected Disease Holes

The average office toilet has 49 germs per square inch. Your office computer keyboard has, on average, 4,000 germs per square inch. But that's nothing compared to your office phone – it has 25,000 germs per square inch. Remember that, next time your too lazy to walk to your boss's office. A virus, such as norovirus, the common cold or stomach flu, can travel around an office in four hours.

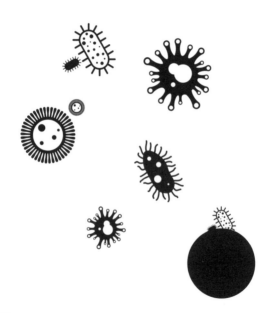

Quote Quota #24

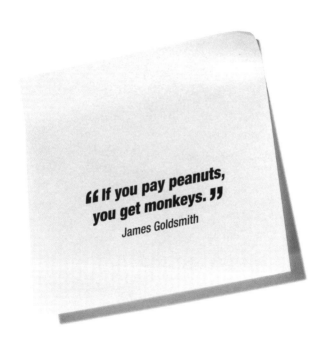

❝ If you pay peanuts, you get monkeys. ❞

James Goldsmith

Quote Quota #62

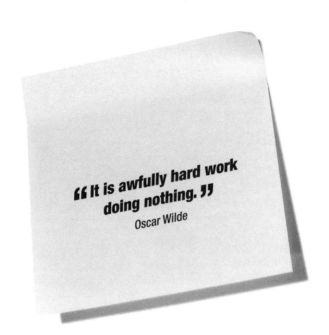

It is awfully hard work doing nothing.

Oscar Wilde

Office Party Rules

We often forget these days that even though office Christmas parties or outings are parties, they are still business events where our behaviour is observed and judged every minute and impressions by gossipy co-workers are constantly made. But sod all that – here are ten tips to having a ball at this year's office do:

1 Wear something raunchy (men and women)

2 Proper snog all your co-workers under the mistletoe

3 Be the first to start the conga. If no one else joins in, keep going

4 Don't drink on an empty stomach – try to keep going all night!

5 Tell everyone how much you hate Dave, the CEO, when Dave is standing right behind you

6 Be the last person to leave – no one can gossip about you then

7 Wait until someone you fancy is leaving, jump in a taxi with them

8 Be the first on the dancefloor. Even if there is no dancefloor

9 Start rumours about co-workers you dislike, and spread them around. Wait for them to come back to you

10 Vomit tactically every few drinks. This will save it erupting out spontaneously all down your clothes

Buzzword Bingo!

The office-based disease currently spreading itself like Avian Flu across the globe goes by a few nasty-sounding nouns – Jargon, Buzzwords, Cliché, Waffle, and so on. In your office, you'll know it by it's true name: bullsh*t. The only cure for this utterly depressing infection is Buzzword Bingo!, a Bingo-style quiz where frustrated office workers (just like you) prepare Bingo cards with corporate buzzwords on them and tick them off when they are spoken during an office-related event, such as a pointless sales call, boring monthly staff meeting or your dreaded one-to-one weekly "catchup" meetings with the boss. The goal is to tick off as many buzzwords as possible and and then yell "Bullsh*t!" as loud as possible. If you haven't worked it out already, the whole point of this game is to let your entire office know when someone in your office is talking complete and utter bullsh*t.

Here's a practice Buzzword Bingo card for you to photocopy and go nuts with:

★ BINGO ★

BANDWIDTH	THINKING FORWARD	BLUE SKY THINKING	VERSION 2.0	TRENDING
HEADS-UP	ACTION	JUDGEMENT CALL	CHECK IN THE BOX	AIR IT OUT
DOWNSIZING	RECRUITING	◯	DROP THE BALL	BRAINSTORM
RISK MANAGEMENT	OUT OF THE LOOP	TOUCH BASE	PROACTIVE	STRATEGY
UNIQUE SELLING PROPOSITION	KEY PERFORMANCE INDICATORS	END-USER PERSPECTIVE	GAME CHANGER	TEAM WORK

How To Avoid Going To A Meeting

Meetings go on and on, don't they? Try these smart and blame-free techniques to get out of meetings now!

1 Simply don't go to begin with. What's the worst that could happen?

2 Don't go – but tell people you were sitting in Meeting Room B, for hours, waiting for people to turn up.

3 Get your mother, friend, or partner to call precisely five minutes into the meeting, and then dash out urgently, as if it's an important life-or-death call.

4 Ask the receptionist to come and get you as soon as the meeting starts because, "there's someone important-looking waiting for you in reception."

5 Tell colleagues that you'll conference call into the meeting, but then start doing crackly and static noises with your mouth and blame the "infernal technology" for not working.

6 Download a Fire Alarm Siren ringtone on your phone, and just as the meeting starts, phone yourself – everyone will think the fire alarm is going off.

7 Start a rumour that you saw a rat in the meeting room, as everyone sits down. Rattle paper under the desk, and shout "There it is!", and jump on your chair.

8 Walk into the meeting very late, but bring biscuits. Everyone will forget that you were late.

9 Create confusion before the meeting starts about whether the meeting is going ahead or not. Then when it does, you can argue legitimately that you thought it wasn't.

10 Sellotape a fresh piece of fish behind the radiator, an hour before the meeting starts. When everyone sits down to start, the stench will be unbearable.

Quote Quota #82

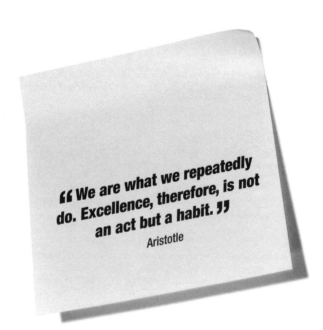

❝ We are what we repeatedly do. Excellence, therefore, is not an act but a habit. ❞

Aristotle

Curb Your Enthusiasm

One way bosses and senior managers seem to get ahead in the workplace is by curbing their enthusiasm to do the work that is offered to them. Here are ten phrases senior staff and managers use on a daily basis, to wriggle out of being decent human beings:

1 "I'm too busy to do that now. It will have to wait. Unless you can do it?"

2 "You start without me, and I'll be along later to see how you're doing."

3 "I've got to leave early to go somewhere important, but you guys carry on."

4 "I just made myself a cup of tea... I assumed you guys were OK without one."

5 "I wasn't involved in this project until it was a success, and now it has everything to do with me."

6 "This project was a success last time I looked at it."

7 "Don't worry, I'll step in and save the day."

8 "At the end of the day, someone is to blame. And that someone isn't me."

9 "It's lunchtime. See you guys tomorrow."

10 "Have a relaxing weekend. Don't forget I need those reports on Monday morning first thing."

Things That Will Make You Cry Today

Eighty per cent of all office workers feel stressed about their jobs, and only 30 per cent feel inspired and engaged about their own careers. These are the root causes of those problems. Which one – if not all – will you encounter today?

1. **Micromanagement**

2. **Lack of career progression and/or promotion**

3. **Job insecurity**

4. **No confidence in management leadership**

5. **Lack of recognition for outstanding work performance**

6. **Poor communication**

7. **Arsehole co-workers**

8. **Boredom**

9. **Deleting an important file; and having to start over**

10. **"A freeze on all salaries for the foreseeable future"**

Office Acronym

What does it all mean? Is there hidden meaning in the word "office"?

Only
Fools
Find
Idiotic
Colleagues
Entertaining

I admit, it's a fairly crap acronym – but can you think of a better one?

Have a go below...

O
F
F
I
C
E

Sense Of Perspective

Perspective is often one of the first things in offices that get jettisoned out of the window when people are overworked. Employees in offices love getting their knickers in a twist over stuff that doesn't matter. Stuff like this:

1 *"If we don't discuss Q2 today, then all hell will break loose."*

2 *"Can somebody else except me please refill the bloody paper tray???!"*

3 *"Somebody else can turn the printers off tonight – I do it every day."*

4 *"Who's got my mug? It was in the kitchen last time I left it."*

5 *"If I don't get that report by end of play, I'll have to alert HR."*

6 *"Why aren't you wearing the name badges corporate asked us all to wear?"*

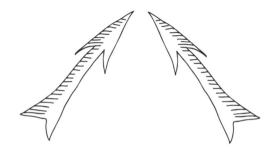

7 *"Our profit margin is down three per cent – who's to blame?"*

8 *"I didn't see you smiling at the office fun day out – you better buck your ideas up if you want to succeed here."*

9 *"If we don't get that report to corporate by 11am exactly, my head will roll."*

10 *"If you don't show up to the meeting it makes me look bad."*

11 *"No one is as busy as me, that's for sure."*

Books To Read
On The Loo

If you want to spend some quality time away from your desk, may I suggest for your reading pleasure the following epic masterpieces? Should you wish, you could disappear on the toilet for weeks at a time with your eyes feasting on their 700+ pages and your trousers around your ankles.

1. *In Search of Lost Time* by Marcel Proust – 4,215 pages

2. *My Struggle* by Karl Ove Knausgård – 3,600 pages

3. *Atlas Shrugged* by Ayn Rand – 1,957 pages

4. *The Lord of the Rings Trilogy* by J.R.R. Tolkien – 1,137 pages

5. *Infinite Jest* by David Foster Wallace – 1,079 pages

6. *The Recognitions* by William Gaddis – 956 pages

7. *1Q84* by Haruki Murakami – 928 pages

8. *Middlemarch* by George Eliot – 904 pages

9. *Anna Karenina* by Leo Tolstoy – 864 pages

10. *The Goldfinch* by Donna Tartt – 784 pages

Office Camouflage

Do you ever wish you could just blend in and not get noticed, especially when your manager needs something doing urgently, because they can't be bothered to do it themselves? Take a leaf out of the books of these creatures below, ten masters of camouflage:

1. **Chameleon**
2. **Stick insect**
3. **Praying mantis**
4. **Elephant hawk moth**
5. **Leaf insect**
6. **Copperband butterfly fish**
7. **King page butterfly**
8. **Crane fly**
9. **Horned toad**

Quote Quota #73

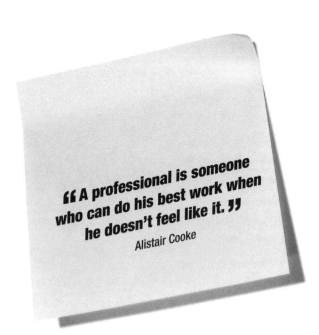

❝ A professional is someone who can do his best work when he doesn't feel like it. ❞

Alistair Cooke

Famous Offices In Movies & TV

One of the most successful places to set a film is in the workplace. Nine out of ten* of them revolve around frustrated, bored and unhappy minions rising up against their evil overlords and taking back their lives. Here are Hollywood unhappiest office drones:

1. **Mr. Incredible,** *The Incredibles*

2. **Narrator,** *Fight Club*

3. **Roy and Moss,** *The IT Crowd*

4. **Chandler Bing,** *Friends*

5. **Tim Canterbury,** *The Office*

6. **Chris,** *Parks and Recreation*

7. **Tess McGill,** *Working Girl*

8. **Ders, Adam & Blake,** *Workaholics*

9. **Michael Bluth,** *Arrested Development*

10. **Homer Simpson,** *The Simpsons*

Minions, ironically, is the obvious exception.

Quote Quota #75

❝ As Mr. Sloan always says, there is no 'I' in team, but there is an 'I' in pie. And there's an 'I' in meat pie. Meat is the anagram of team… I don't know what he's talking about. ❞

Shaun of the Dead, 2004

FYI

A recent survey reported that one out of three employees who received a promotion in 2015 used a coffee mug with the company logo on it. Quick – find a mug with a logo on – and make sure you hide it where no one, not even yourself, will ever find it.

Get Awkward #9

Buy a bulk order of plain baseball caps online. When they arrive, scribble the word "THINKING CAP" on the front. Now, leave a cap on each of your co-workers' desks. Every morning, remind all your colleagues, via email, to put on their thinking caps today.

Quote Quota #81

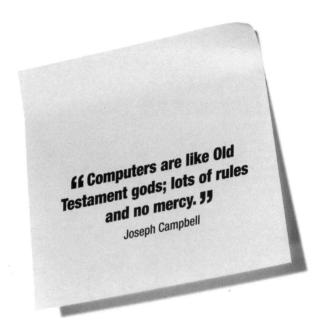

Computers are like Old Testament gods; lots of rules and no mercy.

Joseph Campbell